ASPECTS IN VERSE

POEMS

AVANEESH PRATAP SINGH

Made with ♥ on the Notion Press Platform
www.notionpress.com

Contents

Contents

Foreword

As I read through the poems in "Aspects in Verse," I was struck by the range and depth of the emotions and ideas explored in these pages. From love and romance to success and failure, from family relationships to societal issues, this collection touches on a wide variety of themes that are central to the human experience.

What sets this collection apart is the author's ability to capture these themes in verse that is both accessible and profound. Whether exploring the joys and sorrows of love, the struggles of life, or the complex relationships between family members and society, the author approaches each topic with a sensitive and nuanced understanding that speaks to readers of all ages and backgrounds.

But "Aspects in Verse" is more than just a collection of poems; it is a testament to the power of poetry to move and inspire us. The author's mastery of language and form is evident throughout, as each poem reveals a new facet of the human experience, offering both solace and challenge to the reader.

As you read through these pages, I invite you to journey with the author through the many aspects of life that are captured here, and to find your own reflections and insights within these verses. May these poems serve as a reminder of the richness and complexity of the human experience, and of the enduring power of poetry to help us navigate it.

Priya Singh

Preface

This collection of poems, "Aspects in Verse," represents a journey through the many facets of life and love that have touched me deeply. From the joys and sorrows of romance, to the complexities of family relationships, to the struggles and triumphs of the human spirit, these poems reflect the myriad ways in which we experience the world around us.

Writing poetry has always been a way for me to make sense of my own emotions and experiences, and to connect with others who may share similar feelings or perspectives. In "Aspects in Verse," I hope to offer readers a glimpse into my own journey, as well as a way to reflect on their own experiences and feelings through the lens of poetry.

While the poems in this collection cover a wide range of themes and styles, there are a few common threads that run throughout. One is a deep appreciation for the FRIENDS who were always there, attitude which always enforced me to be a better observer. Another is a recognition of the power of human connection, and the ways in which our relationships with others shape our experiences and our identities, and many more about positives and negatives of life and its complexities.

Ultimately, my hope is that these poems will speak to readers in their own unique ways, offering solace, inspiration, or simply a moment of reflection. Whether you are a longtime lover of poetry, or simply someone seeking a way to make sense of the world, I invite you to join me on this journey through the "Aspects in Verse."

1. LIFE

Life can be tough, it can be a grind,
With challenges at every turn.
But through the hardships, we learn to find
Strength we never knew we had, we learn.
The road may be rough, and the path unclear,
But we keep moving forward, step by step.
With each new obstacle, we conquer our fear,
And rise above the challenges, we prep.
For life is a journey, a test of our will,
A chance to discover who we truly are.
And in the face of adversity, we still
Have the power to rise, to reach for the stars.
So let us embrace the struggles we meet,
And find the courage to carry on.
For it is through these challenges we will complete
The journey of life, where we'll find our dawn.
In the end, we'll look back on our path
And realize the struggles we faced
Were the very things that helped us to laugh,
And embrace the beauty of life's grace.
We'll see that the hardships we overcame,
Were just a small part of the plan,
And that the journey through life's struggles,

Was all worth it, to reach a better stand.
So let us keep moving forward, with hope,
And trust in the journey, the path we take.
For the journey through life's struggles,
Is what helps us grow, and what helps us make.

2. HER TENDERNESS

I want to get lost in your embrace,
Your arms around me in a loving embrace.
I want to feel your warmth and your grace,
Your sweet scent and your gentle caress.
Your beauty entices me, I can't resist,
Your touch, your kiss, your tenderness.
Your sensual gaze, I can't resist,
Your lips so inviting, I can't help but trespass.
Your curves and curves, I can't resist,
Your passionate love that I can't resist.
Your lips so soft, I can't resist,
I want to make love to you and forget the rest.
Your love is like a drug to me,
Your beauty captivates me, I can't break free.
I want to feel your body close to mine,
Your passionate love is pure and divine.

3. FAILURE

Failure is a part of life,
a teacher in disguise,
A chance to learn and grow,
and look towards the skies.
It's not a mark of weakness,
nor a sign of defeat,
But an opportunity,
to rise up off your feet.
For every time we fall,
we rise a little higher,
With new lessons learned, and a little more fire.
We grow in strength and wisdom,
and find a way to win,
And realize that failure,
is just a bump in the road we're in.
So don't be afraid to take risks,
and chase after your dreams,
For it's in the struggles and failures,
that true character beams.
And though the journey may be tough,
and the road may be long,
Remember,success is waiting,
and you're in the right song.

So keep moving forward,
with courage and with grace,
And trust that with each failure,
you'll find a brighter place.
For failure is just a stepping stone,
on the path to your goal,
And in the end,
it's the journey,
that makes us whole.

4. Success is My Only Option

I refuse to falter, I refuse to fall,
For success is my only option, and failure has no place at all.
I will strive with all my might, and reach for the stars above,
For I am determined to succeed, and show the world my love.
I will face each challenge, with a fire in my heart,
And push through every obstacle, with a strength that will not part.
For success is my only option, and I will not be swayed,
By the doubts and fears that try to hold me down each day.
I will rise above it all, and claim my place in the sun,
For I was born to succeed, and my destiny has just begun.
I will not accept defeat, nor will I give in to pain,
For success is my only option, and I will not let it wane.
So I will keep pushing forward, with a heart full of hope,
And I will not let the obstacles, prevent me from my scope.
For success is my only option, and I will not be denied,
I will reach the top, and show the world what I can provide.
So let the journey begin, and let the challenges come,
For I am ready to face them all, with a heart full of courage and a spirit strong.
For success is my only option, and I will never give in,
Until I reach the top, and bask in the glory of my win.

I will not let the naysayers, bring me down with their words,
For I know that I am destined, to achieve all that I've heard.
I will take each step with confidence, and march towards my goal,
For success is my only option, and I will not sell my soul.
I will not be discouraged, by the challenges that I face,
For I know that they are opportunities, to showcase my grace.
I will take each day as it comes, and learn from every mistake,
For success is my only option, and I will not let it break.
I will keep pushing forward, with determination in my heart,
For I know that success is waiting, for me to make a start.
I will not let fear hold me back, nor will I let it win,
For success is my only option, and I will not give in.
I will not be confined, by the limits that others set,
For I know that I am capable, of accomplishing all that's left.
I will reach for the stars above, and climb every mountain high,
For success is my only option, and I will not shy away from the sky.
So I will keep moving forward, with a heart full of hope,
And I will not let the struggles, prevent me from my scope.
For success is my only option, and I will not be denied,
I will reach the top, and bask in the glory of my pride.

5. The Fire Within

There's a fire within you,
a flame that burns bright,
A spark of determination,
shining through the night.
A force that drives you,
to chase your every dream,
A power that's within you,
a brighter than it seems.
It's the voice that whispers,
"Keep pushing, don't you stop,"
It's the drive that keeps you,
always reaching for the top.
It's the courage that you have,
to face the world with grace,
It's the fire within you,
that helps you find your place.
So when life gets tough,
and the road is steep,
And it feels like you're losing,
just remember to keep.
The fire within you,
burning bright and strong,
And soon enough,

you'll be singing a victory song.
For the fire within you,
is your guiding light,
A source of inspiration,
a beacon shining bright.
It's the spark that drives you,
to be your best each day,
And to never give up,
no matter what people say.
So keep the fire within you,
burning bright and true,
And never forget, that
the best is yet to come, through.
For the fire within you,
is a force to be reckoned with,
And with it, you
can do anything, conquer every myth.

6. The Attitude Anthem

I've got an attitude,
and I wear it with pride,
I don't back down,
I don't run and hide.
I stand tall and face
each challenge with grace,
With my head held high,
I show the world my face.
My attitude is sassy,
it's bold and it's free,
It's a reflection of me,
and all that I can be.
I don't let others bring me down,
or dim my light,
I rise above the haters,
and shine brighter every night.
So bring on the drama,
bring on the strife,
I'll take it all on,
with a smile and a life.
For I know that my attitude,
is my greatest asset,
And with it, I'll conquer all,

and never once forget.
So here's to the power of attitude,
the fire in our soul,
Let's embrace it, let's flaunt it,and never let it go.
For we are the masters of our own destiny,
And with a positive attitude, there's nothing we can't be.
With attitude, we don't just,
face the world head on,
We own it, we conquer it,
and we make it our own.
We rise above the negativity,
and the hate that we see,
And we walk with confidence,
and our own unique style and glee.
Attitude gives us the strength,
to face each day with grace,
To tackle every obstacle,
with a smile upon our face.
It's a force that drives us,
to pursue our every goal,
And to never give up,
no matter how big the toll.
Attitude is a beacon, that
guides us through the night,
And helps us find our way,
when the path is not in sight.
It's a source of inspiration,

a fire that we can kindle,
And with it, we can achieve,
all that we set out to middle.
So let's embrace our attitude,
and let it shine through,
And let's never let anyone,
dull the light that shines so true.
For attitude is the key,
to a life that's rich and grand,
And with it, we can overcome,
every obstacle at hand.

7. The Ties

They say that life's a journey, and it's true,
And there are moments, that I'd like to undo.
But then I think of my bros, and I find peace,
For they're the ones who've helped me, to find my release.
They've seen me at my worst, and held me up high,
And never once judged me, or told me goodbye.
They've been there for me, in times of great need,
And always shown me, the love that I need.
They've laughed with me, through the good times and bad,
And always been there, to make me glad.
They've picked me up, when I've fallen down,
And helped me stand tall, when I felt like a clown.
So here's to my bros, the ones who've stood by,
The ones who've held me, when I couldn't fly.
For they're the ones who've shown me, what it means,
To have true friends, and the ties that bind.
For they are my family, my heart and my soul,
The ones who've helped me, to grow and to glow.
And I'm grateful for their love, and the bond we share,
For they are my bros, and I know they'll always be there.
They've been my wingmen, through the ups and the downs,
And never left me, to face life's trials alone.
They've been my strength, when I was feeling weak,

And always cheered me on, when I was feeling meek.
They've shared their lives, and opened up their hearts,
And never once let me, fall apart.
They've stood by me, in the face of adversity,
And shown me what true friendship, and loyalty can be.
So here's to my bros, the ones who are rare,
The ones who've changed my life, and made it more fair.
For they are my brothers, my family, my all,
And I'm proud to have them, as a part of my fall.

8. The Silent Battle

He walks the streets,
with a smile on his face,
Hiding the pain,
that he can't erase.
He's fighting a battle,
that no one can see,
And the weight of it all,
is starting to weigh on him heavily.
He's trying to make it,
in a world that's so tough,
Where the pressure to succeed,
is just too rough.
He's trying to find his place,
in a society that's fast,
And the race to the top,
is leaving him feeling aghast.
He's struggling with self-doubt,
and the fear of the unknown,
And the loneliness that comes,
with being on his own.
He's trying to find his way,
in a world that's so vast,
And the journey ahead,

is just too hard to surpass.
But despite it all,
he still stands tall,
And fights for what's right,
no matter how small.
For he knows deep down,
that he's not alone,
And that one day,
he'll find his way back home.
So let us support him,
and stand by his side,
For he's fighting a battle,
that we can't abide.
And together, we'll help him,
through the storms he must face,
For he's the future of this country,
and a shining star in this place.

9. The Selfish Ones

There are those who come and go,
in our lives like the tide,
They only remember us,
when they're in need of a guide.
They take and take without a thought,
and never give a thing,
And leave us feeling empty,
with a heart that wants to sing.
They are the selfish ones,
who only think of themselves,
And never consider others,
when they're making wealth.
They have no empathy,
no care for those in need,
And leave behind a wake of hurt,
and broken hearts to feed.
So stay away from these ones,
for they will only bring you pain,
And rob you of your happiness,
and drive you insane.
For their love is not true love,
it's merely a facade,
And in the end, it's only you,

who will pay the toll.
So surround yourself with people,
who lift you up with care,
And bring joy to your life,
make you feel they're there.
For these are the ones who matter,
in this world so full of strife,
And they will be with you always,
throughout your journey of life.
So hold your head up high,
and trust in who you are,
And never let the selfish ones,
be the guiding star.
For you are strong and capable,
and have so much to give,
And you deserve the best in life,
to help you truly live.
So seek out those who uplift,
and build you up with love,
And know that in their presence,
you'll soar above.
For these are the ones who matter,
and will always be by your side,
And together, you'll weather life's storms,
and reach for greater heights.
And when the journey's over,
and you look back with pride,

It will be the memories made with the ones,
by your side,
That will shine bright in your heart,
and bring a warm embrace,
And show you that true love,
is what truly makes this place.

10. FAILURE

Failure is a part of life,
a teacher in disguise,
A chance to learn and grow, and look towards the skies.
It's not a mark of weakness,
nor a sign of defeat,
But an opportunity,
to rise up off your feet.
For every time we fall,
we rise a little higher,
With new lessons learned,
and a little more fire.
We grow in strength and wisdom,
and find a way to win,
And realize that failure,
is just a bump in the road we're in.
So don't be afraid to take risks,
and chase after your dreams,
For it's in the struggles and failures,
that true character beams.
And though the journey may be tough,
and the road may be long,
Remember,
success is waiting,

and you're in the right song.
So keep moving forward,
with courage and with grace,
And trust that with each failure,
you'll find a brighter place.
For failure is just a stepping stone,
on the path to your goal,
And in the end,
it's the journey, that makes us whole.

11. JOURNEY OF LIFE

Life can be a cruel mistress,
Sometimes it can be a total mess.
It can be a chaotic journey,
Where you are always on the run.
It can be a heartbreaking struggle,
Where you are always in a muddle.
It can be a path of pain and sorrow,
Where you face hardships and treachery.
It can be a rollercoaster of emotions,
Where you are always in a flux.
It can be a never-ending battle,
Where you are always defeated.
But life is also full of beauty,
Where you can find moments of joy and peace.
It can be a journey of discovery,
Where you find the strength to persevere.

12. YOUR LOVE

I feel your sensual touch in my soul,
Your delicate caress stirs my heart.
Your passionate kiss ignites a fire within me,
My body aches for your embrace.
Your touch is like an elixir to me,
Your embrace is a balm for my soul.
Your gentle kiss is a cure for my pain,
Your love is a sweet potion of joy.
Your soft lips are like honey to me,
Your caress is a gentle breeze.
Your embrace is a sweet embrace of love,
Your kiss is a divine blessing from above.
Your love is like a fire that burns in me,
Your body is a temple of beauty and grace.
Your warmth is like a blanket of comfort,
Your love is a sweet intoxication of joy.

13. MY LOVE

My love for you is like a flame,
That burns and blazes ever so brightly.
It starts in my heart and radiates outward,
To all the corners of my life.
My love for you is like a river,
Flowing ever onward and ever strong.
It erodes away my doubts and fears,
And fills me with endless warmth.
My love for you is like a firework,
Exploding in a bright, vivid display.
It brings joy and beauty to my life,
And creates a spark of passionate desire.
My love for you is like a star,
Shining brightly in the night sky.
It guides me through the darkest hours,
And fills my life with its sparkling light.

14. I'M DONE WITH YOU

I'm done with your lies and excuses,
Your words of deceit, your charades of abuse.
I'm tired of your empty promises,
Your manipulation, your sickening ruse.
I'm done with your hurtful words and games,
Your backstabbing, your lies and sham.
I'm fed up with your mood swings and blame,
Your lack of respect, your lack of care and concern.
I'm done with your insults and put-downs,
Your condescending attitude, your cold, distant frowns.
I'm fed up with your jealous rage,
Your lack of understanding, your self-centeredness, your one-sidedness.
I'm done with your controlling ways,
Your manipulation, your lack of trust.
It's time for me to stand up and say,
"I don't need this, I'm done, I'm done with you."

15. The Brotherhood of Bromance

We stand together, my bros and I,
Through thick and thin, we never say die.
We've laughed and cried, shared joy and pain,
And stood by each other, through every strain.
They say that true friends, are hard to find,
But I'm blessed, to have these bros of mine.
They've been there for me, through every strife,
And lifted me up, in moments of life.
They're my rock, my shield, my trusty crew,
The ones who know me, the ones who know who.
They understand me, when no one else does,
And their love and support, is something I cannot refuse.
So here's to my bros, the ones who stand tall,
The ones who've got my back, and catch me when I fall.
For I know that no matter where life may lead,
They'll always be there, and that's a guarantee.
So here's to the bond of bromance, strong and true,
To the memories we've shared, and the ones yet to come too.
For my bros are more than friends, they're family at heart,
And I'm grateful for their love, right from the very start.

16. MAKE MY WAY

Life throws a lot of struggles my way,
A never-ending uphill battle that I must fight.
It's a war of attrition and perseverance,
A battle against the odds with no respite.
The odds are stacked against me and I'm feeling the strain,
But I will not falter, I will not break.
I'll keep pushing forward and I will remain,
A beacon of hope in an ocean of hate.
The raging storms of life will not deter me,
I will stand firm in the face of adversity.
I'll never surrender, I'll never give up,
I'll continue to strive and never stop.
No matter what life throws my way,
I will stay strong and ride the wave.
I will never succumb to the darkness and despair,
I will remain steadfast and never give up on my dreams.

17. INDIAN YOUTH

The weight of the world,
on their young shoulders,
The future of India, in
their hands, they hold her.
But their path ahead, is
filled with struggles untold,
And the journey ahead,
is far from being old.
They're fighting for their dreams,
in a world that's tough,
Where the odds are against them,
and it's never enough.
They're trying to make a change,
in a system that's flawed,
But their voices go unheard,
and their efforts go awed.
They're burdened by expectations,
and the pressure to perform,
And the fear of failure,
is always there, like a storm.
They're trying to find their place,
in a society that's fast,
Where the race to the top,

is leaving them feeling passed.
They're grappling with issues,
that were once thought of as rare,
Like unemployment, poverty,
and the rising cost of care.
They're trying to stay afloat,
in a world that's drowning,
Where their future is uncertain,
and their dreams are being clowned.
But amidst all this,
they still stand strong,
And fight for what's right,
no matter how wrong.
For they're the future of India,
and they're not alone,
And they'll change the world,
with their courage and their tone.

18. BROKEN HEARTS

Broken hearts,
shattered dreams,
The pain of love,
that's what it seems.
Betrayed by love,
and left all alone,
With nothing but the memories,
that once had flown.
The trust that was given,
was broken in two,
And the wounds of the heart,
they still feel brand new.
The pain of being cheated,
is just too much to bear,
And the memories of love,
are now just a nightmare.
The laughter and joy,
have now turned to tears,
And the hope that was once there,
has disappeared.
The hurt that was caused,
runs deep down inside,
And the wounds of the heart,

are yet to subside.
But amidst all the pain,
there's still a glimmer of hope,
And the strength to move on,
is starting to grow.
For the heart may be broken,
but it's not shattered beyond repair,
And the love that was lost,
will one day reappear.
So hold on to hope,
and have faith in your heart,
And the wounds of the past,
will soon depart.
For love is a journey,
with twists and turns,
And the greatest reward,
is the love that returns.

19. CHEATERS

You thought you could get away,
with breaking a heart,
And leaving behind,
a trail of pain and hurt.
But little did you know,
your actions have a cost,
And the price you'll pay,
will come at a great cost.
You thought love was a game,
to be played with no care,
And that hearts could be broken,
without a second thought or a Fear.
But love is not a toy,
to be played with or tossed,
And the consequences of cheating,
will come at a great cost.
You thought you could hide,
from the truth of your deeds,
And the hurt you've caused,
with your thoughtless and selfish needs.
But the truth will always come out,
and your lies will be exposed,
And the karma of cheating,

will come at a great cost.
beware of the consequences, of cheating in love,
And the pain that you'll cause,
to the ones you once loved.
For the price of your actions,
will come due in full,
And the karma of cheating,
will be the greatest toll.
Your words were sweet,
and your smile was bright,
But your actions have left,
a permanent scar in sight.
The trust that was given,
you threw it away,
left a broken heart,
that will never be the same.
You thought love was easy,
and that you could take,
And leave behind,
a shattered heart in your wake.
But love is not a prize,
to be won or lost,
And cheating in love,
will come at a great cost.
You thought you could run,
from the truth of your lies,
And hide from the pain,

that you left in their eyes.
But the truth will always find,
a way to the light,
And cheating in love,
will come at a great cost.
remember these words,
and heed this advice,
For cheating in love,
will come at a great price.
The consequences of your action,
From Netwon's 3rd law,
has equal reaction.

20. MOTHER'S LOVE

She's the one who nurtured you,
with love and gentle care,
And through all the ups and downs,
she was always there.
With a warm and a soft kiss,
she soothed away your fears,
And dried your tears,
with a comforting touch and a mother's tears.
She's the one who taught you,
the ways of right and wrong,
And showed you the path,
to a life where you belong.
With her unwavering faith,
and her guidance so true,
She helped you to grow,
into the person you are today, too.
She's the one who stood by you,
through every challenge and strife,
And her love was a constant,
throughout every twist of life.
With a gentle voice and a kind heart,
she guided you through the dark,
And her love and her wisdom,

was always there to light your path.
She's the one who sacrificed,
her own dreams and desires,
So that you could live, a life
filled with love, joy, and fire.
And even though she may be far,
her love still shines so bright,
And in your heart and your memories,
her love will always shine, every night.

21. A Teacher's Touch

They shape the minds of youth,
with a gentle hand and care,
And though they may never show it,
they bear a heavy load to bear.
For the knowledge that they impart,
and the lessons that they teach,
Are the building blocks, for
the futures that our students reach.
They are the ones who inspire,
with a spark of creativity,
And their passion for their subject,
is what sets them apart, you see.
With their love for learning,
and their endless supply of grace,
They guide us on our journey,
and help us find our place.
They are the ones who listen,
and offer a shoulder to lean on,
their kindness and their wisdom,
are what make them truly strong.
With their unwavering support,
and their steadfast belief in us,
They help us to believe in ourselves,

and to rise above.
They are the ones who challenge,
and push us to be our best,
And their expectations,
are what help us to stand the test.
With their gentle guidance,
and their tough but fair demands,
We reach our full potential,
and able to take a stand.
They are the ones who shape us,
mold us into who we are,
their influence and their teachings,
will stay with us near and far.
With their dedication and their love,
they make a lasting impact,
their wisdom and guidance,
will always have a firm grasp.

22. FATHER

He's the one who stands tall,
with a quiet strength and grace,
And though he may never show it,
he wears a weary face.
For the burdens that he bears,
and the battles that he fights,
Are a silent sacrifice,
for the ones he loves with all his might.
He's the one who works hard,
to provide a better life,
And though he may never say it,
he bears the greatest strife.
With a smile on his face,
and a twinkle in his eye,
He hides his pain and emotions,
sacrifices just to see you high.
He's the one who teaches you,
the values that you hold,
his love and his guidance,
will always keep you bold.
With his unwavering spirit,
and his steadfast resolve,
He shows you the way,

to a life filled with love, hope, and soul.
He's the one who stands by you,
through every trial and test,
his love and his support,
are always at their best.
With his quiet courage,
his strong and steady hand,
He shows you the way,
to a life filled with strength, honor, and stand.
He's the one who nurtures you,
with a love that knows no bounds,
And his gentle presence,
will always calm you down.
With his wisdom and his guidance,
he leads you to the light,
his unwavering love,
will shine bright, day and night.
He's the one who encourages you,
to chase your dreams with pride,
And his support and his belief,
will always be by your side.
With his sacrifice and his love,
he gives you the courage to soar,
And his wisdom and his guidance,
will guide you to the shore.

23. Bridging the Divide

In a world that's filled with hate,
and violence in our streets,
It's hard to see a brighter future,
where love and peace can meet.
For the rise of inter-religious tension,
is a cause for great concern,
the flames of bigotry and hatred,
seem to always burn.
But we cannot let this divide,
continue to spread its fire,
We must come together,
seek a way to quell its desire.
For though our beliefs may differ,
our paths may be apart,
We must remember, that at our core,
we are all a single heart.
We are bound by our humanity,
the things that make us whole,
And we must work together,
to heal the wounds that we have caused.
In a world that's growing smaller,
with each passing day,
We cannot afford to let our differences,

lead us all astray.
We must find a way to bridge this divide,
to build a better way,
Where love and compassion,
can lead us all astray.
Where our differences are celebrated,
and our unity is strong,
And where peace and harmony,
can right the wrongs.
So let us reach out our hands,
join together in the fight,
To create a world where love,
kindness, are the guiding lights.
Where everyone is welcome,
and everyone is free,
And where our humanity,
is the only thing that we all see.
For in the end,
it's not our beliefs, or cultures that define,
But it's our actions, our kindness,
that will help us all to shine.
So let us come together,
and embrace a brighter day,
Where love and unity,
will help us pave the way.

24. The Struggle Within

Life is a battle, full of twists and turns,
A journey filled with struggles, that often burn.
But we must not falter, nor let our spirit bend,
For every obstacle, is an opportunity to mend.
It's easy to surrender, and give up on the fight,
But true strength lies in the ability to keep things bright.
For every challenge, is a chance to grow,
And every struggle, is an opportunity to show.
The fire within us, the strength that we hold,
The power to rise above, the courage to be bold.
For every defeat, is just a step towards success,
And every setback, is just a means to progress.
So hold your head high, and keep your eyes on the prize,
For every moment of doubt, is just an opportunity to rise.
For life is a journey, that we must face with grace,
And every obstacle, is just another test of our faith.
So embrace the struggle, with a smile and a nod,
For every challenge, is just a means to grow.
And never give up, until that struggle surrenders,
For a life well-lived, is a life well-remembered

25. DEAREST LOVE

My dearest love, my sweetest rose,
With beauty that no one knows.
Your eyes of sparkles, like morning dew,
Your voice so soft, it mesmerizes me too.
Your laugh as pure as crystal clear,
Your heart so kind, no one could compare.
Your love is gentle, like a spring breeze,
Your touch so warm, it fills me with ease.
Your beauty is more than just skin deep,
Your spirit so strong, no one could ever keep.
Your courage and strength that I admire,
Your inner beauty, I could never tire.
My love for you will never fade,
Your beauty and strength will never be replaced.
Your love is my forever joy,
love, you are my world's one and only foy.

My heart sings of love's sweetest melody
for the one who brightens up my day,
Your beauty lights up the night so brightly
Your beauty takes my breath away.

Your gentle spirit glows so brightly

Your tender touch sends shivers through me,
Your laugh is like a sweet song in the night
Your warm embrace lights up my sea.
Your strength and grace I find so endearing
Your kind heart sets my soul on fire,
Your gentle soul soothes my weary soul
Your love is my one true desire.
Your beauty, grace and love are my treasure
My heart soars for you each passing day,
Your smile is the sweetest thing I have ever seen
My love for you will never fade away.

About The Author

Avaneesh Pratap Singh

Avaneesh Pratap Singh is an emerging poet with a passion for exploring the many aspects of the human experience through the medium of poetry. Born and raised in [Ghazipur District,India], Avaneesh discovered a love of words at a young age, and has been honing their craft ever since.

After earning a degree in Master's In Chemistry, Avaneesh Pratap Singh began writing poetry in earnest, drawing inspiration from personal experiences, nature, and the beauty of language itself. His poetry explores themes of love and loss, family relationships, and the joys and struggles of everyday life, with a keen eye for detail and a deep appreciation for the many mysteries of the human spirit.

In addition to writing poetry, Avaneesh Pratap Singh is also an avid reader, Humanitarian and a lover of the outdoors. When not immersed in the world of words, they can often be found exploring local bookstores, or spending time with family and friends.

"Aspects in Verse" is Avaneesh Pratap Singh's first collection of poetry, and represents a culmination of years of hard work, passion, and dedication. It is their hope that these poems will touch the hearts and minds of readers, and inspire others to explore the beauty and complexity of the world around us.

9 798889 754909

Printed by Libri Plureos GmbH in Hamburg, Germany